FIRE

and Other Bible Stories You've Got to Hear!

ON FIRE

and Other Bible Stories You've Got to Hear!

IRENE HOWAT

CF4•K

DEDICATION
For Alasdair

10 9 8 7 6 5 4 3 2 1
© Copyright 2012 Christian Focus Publications
ISBN 978-1-84550-780-0

Published in 2012 by
Christian Focus Publications, Geanies House, Fearn, Tain,
Ross-shire, IV20 1TW, U.K.
Text by Irene Howat

Cover design by Daniel van Straaten
Cover illustration and inside illustrations
by Fred Apps
Printed and bound by Bell and Bain, Glasgow

Scripture quotations are based on the HOLY BIBLE, NEW
INTERNATIONAL VERSION®. NIV®. Copyright©1973, 1978,
1984 by International Bible Society. Used by permission of
Zondervan. All rights reserved.

CONTENTS

NO WAY BACK

What's the first thing you do when someone shouts fire? You run! And fast. This book is all about fires – and we're not going to run away from them. In fact, we're going to get as close as we can to the fires to see what was actually happening.

We are going on a journey back in time to the very first fire that we know about. This fire is in the Garden of Eden where Adam and Eve lived after

God created them. It's quite difficult to imagine Eden because what happened there changed the world so much. But let's try.

Everything is good and peaceful and happy. There is no sickness or sadness. Nobody grows old and nobody dies. Adam and Eve are always in the best of health. They never argue or fight. Lions don't eat zebras and cats don't chase mice. Everything in Eden is perfect. Best of all, Adam and Eve have God's presence there. Because they have never done anything wrong, neither of them has a guilty conscience and they are able to really enjoy being with God in their wonderful garden home.

Imagine seeing a butterfly for the first time and then think of turning a corner and nearly walking into the first giraffe you've ever seen! Now think of the tastes you'd enjoy – mangoes and pineapples, bananas and sun-warmed peaches.

That was what the Garden of Eden was like until a truly terrible thing happened. God had told Adam and Eve that there was a tree in the middle of the garden called the Tree of the Knowledge of Good and Evil, and they were not to eat the fruit of that tree. If they ate the fruit, they would die. No problem! Adam and Eve had every other tree you can imagine ... and many you can't!

However, one day Satan came in the form of a serpent and spoke to Eve. Listen to what was said.

'Did God really say, "You must not eat from any tree in the garden?"' the serpent asked Eve.

Of course God hadn't said that and Eve should have told him so.

'We may eat fruit from the trees in the garden,' she replied, 'but God did say, "You must not eat fruit from the tree that is in the middle of the garden, and you must not touch it, or you will die."

9

Oops! Did God really say that they hadn't to touch the fruit? He did not! Eve hadn't been paying attention. And we should never make up things and say that God said them.

'You will not surely die,' Satan argued.

This was a lie, and Satan knew it. He went on to say that God knew that if they ate the forbidden fruit, they'd know good from evil and be just like God! Satan is clever at telling half truths that are

really lies, and this was one of them. Yes, Adam and Eve would know good from evil, but they certainly wouldn't be like God.

You know that Eve should have turned away from the tree, but she didn't. She looked at it. Foolish woman. She thought about it. Foolish, foolish woman. Then she stretched out her hand, picked a fruit and ate it. Not only that, she gave some to Adam and he ate it too. Because Eve listened to Satan rather than God she and Adam did something that changed human history.

For the very first time Adam and Eve felt guilt and embarrassment. They tried to hide from God but that's not possible. When God asked Adam what had happened, he blamed Eve. He even blamed God because God had given him Eve who had caused all the trouble! Eve passed the blame to Satan. Suddenly all the beauty of their lives was one horrible mess.

All three, Adam, Eve and Satan, were punished. Adam was told that he would have to work very hard in difficult conditions to make things grow. Eve was told that being a wife and mother would cause her hurt and pain. The serpent was told that someone was going to come who would crush him. And here's an interesting thing about the serpent. God said that from then on the serpent would crawl on its belly so it must have had legs before that!

This is where the fire comes in. Adam and Eve were sent out of Eden and an angel with a fiery sword was sent by God as a guard to prevent them getting back in. The fire that flashed from the angel's sword is the first fire that is mentioned in the Bible. It was a truly terrible fire for it prevented Adam and Eve from ever getting back into Eden. By their sin they brought sadness and sickness and death into the world. What God had told them was absolutely true.

Do you remember that when God cursed the serpent he said that *someone* would come who would crush him? That *someone* came many years later and he is the Lord Jesus Christ. Nobody has ever been able to get back into Eden, but those who trust in Jesus go to heaven when they die and that is even better. No fiery sword can keep Christians out of heaven because God has promised them a home there.

We can't use our imaginations to go to heaven, but we can read about it in the Bible. There God tells us what it will be like for everyone who trusts in Jesus. They will be God's people, 'and God himself will be with them and be their God. He will wipe every tear from their eyes. There will be no more death or mourning or crying or pain, for the old order of things has passed away.'

(This story is found in Genesis 3 and Revelation 21:3-4.)

BURNING BUT NOT BURNT

The problem about fire is that it burns things up. Our second trip back in time takes us to a bush that blazed but didn't burn up at all! Are you ready to go there?

Imagine you are watching a scene playing out on a hillside covered with scrub. As it's in the Middle East there will probably be bushes rather than big trees and the grass will be rather thin.

On Fire

There's a shepherd on the hillside. Because of the thin grass he has to move his flocks day by day to make sure they have enough to eat. That's what this shepherd, Moses, is doing. Suddenly Moses sees something strange, so strange that he goes to investigate. Use your imagination to see and to hear what happened.

Moses sees a bush on fire, not just smouldering and smoking, for he can actually see the flames. Even from a distance Moses can see that, while the flames are raging, the bush isn't burning up!

'I will go over and see this strange sight – why the bush does not burn up,' thinks Moses.

So the shepherd walks from his sheep to the burning bush. As he nears the bush, God's voice speaks to him from out of the flames!

'Moses!' God calls. 'Moses!'

Just imagine his surprise.

'Here I am,' he answers.

God's voice speaks again from out of the burning bush.

'Do not come any closer,' he says. 'Take off your sandals, for the place where you are standing is holy ground.'

Of course it is holy ground because God is there!

Moses takes off his sandals.

The bush continues to burn right in front of Moses. He must feel the heat from it even though the leaves aren't as much as charred.

Moses listens as God explains who he is.

'I am the God of your father, the God of Abraham, the God of Isaac and the God of Jacob.'

When Moses hears who is speaking to him, he covers his face for he is afraid to see God. Imagine his amazement and fear as God continues to speak to him.

To understand what God says to Moses you need a one hundred-word history lesson.

God had chosen a people (the Israelites) for himself but, many years before, they had gone to Egypt for food during a bad famine. Now God's people were kept in Egypt by Pharaoh as slaves. They were treated terribly cruelly and day after day they cried out to God for help. Moses was an Israelite and God had saved him from slavery in order that he could lead his people out of Egypt. But Moses did not yet know that. In fact, Moses had run away from Egypt because he killed an Egyptian who had been abusing an Israelite man.

That was exactly one hundred words!

As the fire continued to blaze, here is what Moses heard God say to him.

'I have indeed seen the misery of my people in Egypt. I have heard them crying out because of their slave drivers, and I am concerned about their suffering. So I have come down to rescue them from the hand of the Egyptians and to bring them up out of that land to a good and spacious land, a land flowing with milk and honey … So now, go. I am sending you to Pharaoh to bring my people the Israelites out of Egypt.'

Just imagine how Moses felt when he heard that. He'd killed an Egyptian and no doubt a warrant was out for his arrest. But the fire blazed and the conversation continued.

'Who am I, that I should go to Pharaoh and bring the Israelites out of Egypt?' asked Moses.

'I will be with you ...' God promised.

Moses was astonished but could only see problems.

'Suppose I go to the Israelites and say to them, "The God of your fathers has sent me to you," and they ask me, "What is his Name?" Then what shall I tell them?'

God replied to Moses, 'I am who I am. This is what you are to say to the Israelites, I AM has sent me to you.'

Having given Moses his precious Name, God outlined his plan. But Moses stood by the burning bush full of doubts and fears.

'What if they don't believe me?' he worried.

God gave him signs of his power.

'Lord, I'm slow of speech and tongue ... Please send someone else,' pleaded Moses.

God told him that he could take his brother, Aaron, with him.

So it is that out of the flaming fires of a bush Moses was told how his people would be rescued.

When God makes plans he carries them out, even if it seems to us to be in strange ways. Moses went to Pharaoh and asked him to let God's people go. Pharaoh would have none of it. Instead, he made the people work even harder in even worse conditions. Things seemed to be going from bad to worse. Moses went right back to God to complain.

'O Lord, why have you brought trouble upon the people? Is this why you sent me? Ever since I went to Pharaoh to speak in your name, he has brought trouble upon this people, and you have not rescued your people at all.'

God didn't criticize Moses for what he said. Rather he explained what was going to happen.

21

'Now you will see what I will do to Pharaoh: Because of my mighty hand he will let them go; because of my mighty hand he will drive them out of his country.'

That's exactly what happened. God sent nine terrible plagues on Egypt and during each one Pharaoh asked Moses to pray for the plague to stop, promising that the Israelites could go free. But, cheat that Pharaoh was, when each plague stopped he changed his mind and kept his slaves.

But after the tenth and most terrible plague of all he did exactly what God had said he would do and Pharaoh actually demanded that the Israelites leave Egypt!

God kept the promise he made to Moses at the burning bush and was with him for the next forty years as he led the Israelites to the land he had promised. It wasn't that it was so very far away, rather that God had many lessons to teach them before they arrived there for they were an ungrateful lot! When they eventually reached the River Jordan, and were ready to cross over into the land God was to give them, the Lord allowed Moses to see it from the top of a nearby hill and then took him home to heaven. Moses didn't actually set foot in the promised land but he led God's people there. Instead Moses went home to heaven which is far, far better.

(This story is found in Exodus 3.)

STOP COMPLAINING!

During the time it took God's people to go from Egypt to the land God had promised to give them they behaved like very spoiled children. In Egypt they had been slaves and were treated terribly cruelly. That's why they wanted to leave. But listen to them complaining to Moses when they were just a short way into their journey.

'If only we had died by the Lord's hand in Egypt. There we sat around pots of meat and ate all the food we wanted, but you have brought us out into this desert to starve this entire assembly to death.'

What short memories they had!

Imagine you had been a young Israelite in Egypt. Your truthful description of what it was like would have been something like this.

'The Egyptians set slave masters over us and they worked us ruthlessly. They made our lives miserable in all kinds of hard labour in the fields. Not only that, they ordered us to make bricks without giving us straw to make them with and then they whipped us when they fell apart! And when we gathered our own straw, whipped us for not making enough bricks on time! They hated us so much that when boy babies were born we were ordered to drown them in the River Nile.'

So much for sitting around pots of meat and eating all the food they wanted!

Despite their grumbling, God did a wonderful thing. He gave them food from heaven!

God said to Moses, 'I will rain down bread from heaven for you. The people are to go out each day and gather enough for that day.'

The food from heaven came in the form of flakes that tasted like wafers with honey and a touch of olive oil! So the ungrateful freed slaves were fed with honey and oil flavoured wafers each day from then on. Now here's something interesting. The people called the flakes 'manna', and the word manna means in their language, 'What is it?' You can just imagine the first morning they went out and the ground was all covered with flakes. The people would have looked at each other and asked, 'What is it?' or 'Manna' in their own language. And the name stuck! But

… needless to say … before long they were at it again. Complaining. Groaning. Moaning.

You would think God would just have abandoned them, stopped the manna and let them die in the desert. They certainly deserved it. Instead, he did a very wonderful thing. A cloud accompanied the people all through their journey. The cloud could be seen clearly in daylight and at night it became a cloud (or pillar) of fire, which could be easily seen in the dark. The cloud was the sign of God's presence with his people. And he used the cloud to show Moses when they were to stay where they were, when they were to move camp, in which direction they were to travel and when they were to stop! The cloud wasn't a satellite navigation system; it was the presence of the King of kings!

Use your imagination to join the people on their long journey. You are in a vast desert and it's the middle of the night. You begin to worry that Moses doesn't really know what he's doing and that you're absolutely lost. Then you look out of your tent and what do you see? You see a fiery cloud in the sky and you know that God is with you. The next morning you hear a discussion.

'Are we going to move camp today or are we here for a while?' someone asks.

'I don't know,' is the answer. 'We'll have to wait to see how we're led.'

The cloud stays put all day, and the next day, and the next day too and you stay where you are. But the following morning the cloud lifts and begins to move. You strike camp, check that all your family is there and get ready to follow the moving cloud in whatever direction it goes. Some nights you don't sleep and the middle of the night is the worst time for worrying. So you look out and your worrying calms, for the fiery cloud is still there. God is still with you. It's all right.

God was very patient, but he is not patient forever. One day the people were at it again. Let's imagine what the conversation could have been like...

'This is awful. I'm sick of deserts. I'd rather be back home in Egypt any day,' grumbles a woman.

Her friend agrees. 'It wasn't so bad in Egypt,' she lies. 'There was always plenty of food, and it wasn't this manna stuff. If I never see manna again, it will be too soon. I've had enough manna to fill me up to here,' she says, tapping the top of her head.

Her friend nods. 'When we reach the promised land I'll never put manna in my mouth, ever!'

Grumble, grumble ... murmer, murmer ... complain, complain ...

God had had enough and he was angry. Fire from the Lord came on the camp and burned among the people. Not only that, but it burned some of the tents around the outside of the camp!

'Pray for us!' the people shouted to Moses, terrified that the fire was going to rage through the whole camp and destroy them all.

Moses prayed to the Lord and the fire died down. The people gave that place in the desert a name. It was called *Taberah*, which means 'burning'.

Despite God leading them with the fiery cloud, despite him feeding them with manna, the complaining still went on!

'If only we had meat to eat!' the people wailed. 'We remember the fish we ate in Egypt at no cost (oh really!!!!!) also the cucumbers, melons, leeks, onions and garlic.'

You'd have thought they'd been in a holiday camp. They had actually been slaves. Still God was good to them and he sent flocks of quails (little birds that taste good) to land in the camp. There was plenty for them all to have meat to eat.

Imagine you are there. Wouldn't you feel wonderful? After all, you'd been freed from slavery. You were on a journey to a country God was going to give you, and you were well fed. No. That's not how they felt. They took every chance they could find to moan and groan.

Once, when there was a temporary shortage of water, they were back to their grumbles again. Poor Moses was really frustrated listening to them!

'Why did you bring us up out of Egypt to make us and our children and livestock die of thirst?'

'If only we had died in Egypt! Why is the Lord bringing us to this land only to let us fall by the sword?'

Were they being killed with swords? Well … no.

'We should choose a leader and go back to Egypt ...' the people went on.

Moses must have been tearing his hair out!

Day by day the cloud stayed still or moved to show the people where to go. Night by night the fiery cloud stayed over them, showing them that, despite their moaning and groaning, God was still with them. And that went on for a whole forty years, so long that the generation that left Egypt died and was buried and a new generation crossed over the River Jordan into the land God had promised to give them.

(This story is found in Exodus 16 and 17, and Numbers 9:15-11:6.)

FIRE FROM HEAVEN

Most fires start with a spark and then go on to flicker before bursting into blazing flames. The Bible tells the story of a very different fire, a very, very different fire!

Imagine you are in the royal palace in Israel over 800 years before Jesus was born. There is a problem. King Ahab, a bad man was married to an even worse wife, Queen Jezebel. They are the 'baddies' in the story. The 'goodie' is Elijah, one of God's prophets. Queen Jezebel has persuaded her spineless husband to encourage the worship of her idol, Baal, among the chosen people of God. The Lord is not pleased and he sends Elijah to do something about it. Elijah is just an ordinary man but God gives him an extraordinary job to do. God's like that.

Elijah heads for the royal palace.

'Is that you, you troubler of Israel?' asks King Ahab.

Not exactly a polite welcome!

'I have not made trouble for Israel,' Elijah replies. 'But you and your father's family have.'

Ahab doesn't like that.

'Now,' says Elijah, with a note of challenge in his voice, 'summon the people from all over Israel to meet me on Mount Carmel. And bring the 450 prophets of Baal and the 400 prophets of Asherah, who eat at Jezebel's table.'

And that's exactly what happens. You find yourself with a huge crowd of people at Mount Carmel. Elijah stands up in front of all the people, he is shouting to be heard.

'How long will it take you to make up your minds about who the true God is? If the Lord is God, follow him; but if Baal is God, follow him.'

There is silence. Over 800 people stand there not knowing what to say. But one man knows what to say, and that is Elijah.

Looking at the 450 prophets of Baal, he tells them to get two bulls to be used as burnt offerings.

'You cut one of them up for an offering,' he tells them. 'Build an altar with great piles of wood for a fire, and put the meat on it … but don't set it alight.'

Imagine the prophets of Baal. Why on earth, they're wondering, does Elijah want them to sacrifice to Baal when he doesn't believe in him?

Elijah is still speaking, and they strain to hear what he's saying.

'I'll prepare the other bull for an offering,' he shouts.

Looking at their puzzled faces, he goes on, 'And then you call on Baal and I'll call on the Lord and we'll see who sends down fire from heaven to burn up the offering.'

It's a competition! The 450 prophets of Baal think it's a great idea and start to prepare their offering.

Let's find out what happened.

One bull was slaughtered and, while some of the prophets of Baal were cutting it up and preparing to offer it to their idol god, many others were gathering wood to make a fire ready for Baal to set it alight with a spark from heaven. Eventually everything was ready. The fire was laid, the great pieces of the bull's carcass were placed on it and the 450 men were ready. Can you imagine their excitement? Would Baal send a spark from heaven, or a thunder bolt, or lightning?

For several hours the prophets of Baal yelled to their god to send fire. They danced round the altar they'd built, shouting, 'O Baal, answer us!' From morning until lunchtime the display went on, getting more and more frenzied with the passage of time.

'Shout louder!' Elijah teased them. 'Maybe Baal's deep in thought, or busy, or away travelling. If he's sleeping, you'll have to scream even louder to waken him up!'

The 450 men shouted louder and even louder. Then they took their spears and swords and started to slash themselves. With blood flowing from them their yells and screams to Baal could be heard for miles ... but they weren't heard by Baal for he doesn't exist!

All afternoon the shouting and dancing, the blood-letting and stamping continued and no thunderbolt was thrown from heaven, no lightning flashed to light the fire. The only sparks that flew were from the prophets' swords and none of them landed on the fire to light it.

By evening Elijah probably didn't have to shout to be heard for the 450 prophets of Baal must have been hoarse!

'Come here,' he said, and they came. They watched as God's prophet Elijah did a most extraordinary thing. Imagine you are on the mountain...

Elijah takes twelve large stones and builds an altar.

Then, with a spade, he begins to dig a ditch all around it.

'What's he doing?' the prophets of Baal wonder.

They watch as he lays wood on the altar – though some of them are struggling to keep their eyes open after the day they've had.

They watch as he slaughters the bull, cuts it up and places the pieces on the wood – though some of them are yawning with exhaustion.

But there isn't a sleepy eye on the mountain when they hear Elijah giving instructions for four great jars of water to be poured over the offering and the wood!

'That will never burn!' they think to themselves. 'He's crazy!'

'Pour over another four great jars of water,' Elijah says.

The prophets of Baal are amazed!

'And another four!'

The water soaks the bull, the wood, the stones and the ditch is running full!

This is just the kind of comedy show the prophets of Baal want after their terrible day.

The time of sacrifice comes and Elijah steps forward.

'O Lord, God of Abraham, Isaac and Israel,' says Elijah in prayer, 'let it be known today that you are God in Israel and that I am your servant and have done all these things at your command. Answer me, O Lord, answer me, so these people will know that you, O Lord, are God, and that you are turning their hearts back again.'

There is no loud shouting, no dancing, no screaming. Elijah doesn't slash himself and get into a frenzy. He just prays … and the fire of the Lord falls and burns up the soaking sacrifice! It burns up the soaking wood! And the flames even burn the stones and the soil below them and lick up every drop of water from the ditch!

What are all the people doing who came to watch the competition? They are flat out on the ground worshipping God! But not the prophets of Baal. They are seized and put to death and their god, who is an idol and not a god, can do nothing whatever to help them.

And that should have been the end of that. King Ahab and Queen Jezebel should have seen God's hand in what happened. They didn't. When Ahab told his wicked wife all about it, she swore that she'd put Elijah to death. Foolish woman! She was really fighting against God himself, not just his prophet, and nobody can fight the God who can send fire from heaven, and win.

(This story is found in 1 Kings 16:16-46.)

BIBLE VERSE

And God spoke all these words:
... You shall not make for yourself
an idol in the form of anything
in heaven above or on the earth
beneath or in the waters below.
You shall not bow down to them
or worship them; for I, the LORD
your God, am a jealous God,
punishing the children for the sin
of the fathers to the third and
fourth generation of those who hate
me, but showing love to a thousand
generations of those who love me and
keep my commandments.

Exodus 20: 1-6

HOTTER THAN HOT!

Imagine yourself in Babylon around 500 years before Jesus was born. You are a soldier in the army and you're talking to another soldier in King Nebuchadnezzar's guard. You are discussing what's happening in the country.

'Have you seen the new statue yet?' you ask him.

Your friend laughs. 'You can hardly miss it, twenty-seven metres high and solid gold! It must have cost millions to make!'

You shake your head.

'And have you heard the King's latest orders?'

'Yes,' says your friend. 'As soon as we hear music we've to bow down and worship his golden statue.'

'Do we have to do that?' you ask. 'What if you believe in just one god, and your god doesn't allow you to worship idols.'

'You'll do it if you want to live,' the other soldier says. 'And if you don't, apparently the King will have you thrown into a blazing furnace. I tell you, if it was me, I'd be down on my knees in front of the statue. Burning to death would not be a good career move!'

You turn around and in the distance you see three men … they seem like friends … they are Shadrach, Meshach and Abednego.

These three friends, Shadrach, Meshach and Abednego are not Babylonians. They are Jews (God's chosen people) and were captured and brought to Babylon as young men, probably teenagers. Over the years they have been well fed, well educated and well trained. They now serve the King, obeying his orders apart from when he asks them to do something that is forbidden in God's law. Bowing down and worshipping a statue is totally and absolutely forbidden. God's law says that only the one living and true God is to be worshipped. The King knows the three men and respects them, which is why they have good government jobs.

Keep thinking of yourself as a member of the King's guard. One day, shortly after the statue is put up, some of the King's wise men arrive at court.

'O King, live for ever!' they say. 'You made a law saying that when music plays everyone who hears it has to bow down and worship your statue of gold.'

The King nods his head.

One of the wise men goes on. 'There are some Jews to whom you have given important jobs, and they are paying no attention to your command. They don't serve your gods and they don't fall down and worship your golden statue when they hear the sound of music.'

King Nebuchadnezzar is angry. In fact, King Nebuchadnezzar is absolutely furious! You wait to see what happens.

'Bring Shadrach, Meshach and Abednego to me!' commands the King.

You and some other soldiers march off to obey his order and return with the three men.

'Is it true,' the King asks, 'that you don't worship my golden statue when you hear the music? I warn you, if it is, you will be thrown into a blazing furnace where no god will help you.'

The three men stand before the King, strong and unafraid.

'If we are thrown into the flaming furnace,' they say, 'our God is able to save us. He will rescue us, O King.'

Just try to imagine how angry King Nebuchadnezzar is!

The men go on. 'But even if God doesn't save us, we will not serve your gods or worship your golden statue.'

Nebuchadnezzar is one very, very furious king! 'Heat that furnace seven times hotter than usual!' he commands.

You watch as Shadrach, Meshach and Abednego are tied up and taken out of the royal presence to be burnt. It takes a little while to heat the furnace, but the job is done as soon as possible. It's not a good idea to keep an angry king waiting. You are detailed to accompany the three men to the furnace, and the King is there too, ready and waiting.

'Throw them in!' he orders furiously.

Some of the other soldiers take Shadrach, Meshach and Abednego by the arms and push them into the raging heat of the furnace. Suddenly screaming fills the air. It's not the three Jews, but the men who pushed them in! The heat is so intense at the mouth of the furnace that they are on fire! Nothing can be done for them. The soldiers are killed almost instantly. You are mightily glad that you aren't one of them.

King Nebuchadnezzar is sitting far enough back to be out of danger. Still raging, he watches carefully to make sure that Shadrach, Meshach and Abednego are burnt to death. Suddenly the king is on his feet, staring into the white heat.

'Wasn't it three men that we tied up and threw into the fire?' he demands.

'Certainly, O King,' you reply.

On Fire

His gaze is fixed on the mouth of the furnace. Nebuchadnezzar shields his face from the heat and stares for as long as he can stand the glare.

'Look!' he shouts, above the roar of the flames. 'I see four men walking in the fire, unbound and unharmed. The fourth looks like a son of the gods!'

The King moves gingerly towards the furnace and shouts in the opening.

'Shadrach, Meshach and Abednego, servants of the Most High God, come out! Come here!'

The three men walk out of the fire! You watch as everyone crowds around them, and you are amazed, utterly amazed. Their clothes are not even singed. The bodies of the men who were killed in the heat of the fire are still lying there, but the three who were actually in the fire don't even have a hair of their head the least bit burned! And, astounded, you notice that they don't even smell of smoke!

All anger has left the King, almost as if it melted in the heat of the flames. You watch his face. He's looking puzzled, amazed and ... you can't quite work out what his expression says.

King Nebuchadnezzar speaks.

'Praise be to the God of Shadrach, Meshach and Abednego, who has sent his angel and rescued his servants! They trusted in him and defied my command. They were willing to give up their lives rather than serve any god but their own God.'

You are careful that your mouth doesn't fall open with surprise. Is this King Nebuchadnezzar speaking? It is, but it certainly doesn't sound like him! You listen carefully to what he says.

'If anyone, from any country, says anything against the God of Shadrach, Meshach and Abednego, he will be cut to pieces and his house knocked down to a pile of stones, for no other god can save the way their God saved them,' announces Nebuchadnezzar.

News soon spreads about what has happened and nobody is in the least surprised that Shadrach, Meshach and Abednego are promoted to better jobs in Babylon. This sets you thinking and you decide that a golden statue can't do anything for anyone. It's only a lump of metal, an idol. But the true and living God is powerful and able to do whatever he chooses to do, even walk in a fire to save his faithful servants from burning.

(This story is found in Daniel 3.)

BIBLE VERSE

Praise be to the name of God for
ever and ever; wisdom and power
are his. He changes times and
seasons; he sets up kings
and deposes them.
He gives wisdom to the wise and
knowledge to the discerning.

Daniel 2:20-21

CAUGHT IN THE FIRELIGHT

A gathering round a fire can be a happy occasion. Perhaps you've sat singing and playing games around a campfire. Or maybe you've had a bonfire barbecue with food cooking in foil as the heat died down. Or you might have helped build an autumn bonfire of garden rubbish and have finished it off with marshmallows toasted in the heat of the embers.

On Fire

The fire in this story was not burning on a happy occasion. In fact, it is probably one of the saddest fire stories in the whole of history. But before we go there we need to visit a place called the upper room. Jesus and the disciples have just celebrated a special meal together there. He makes it perfectly clear to Peter and the others that he is going to die. Peter however, doesn't want that to happen. He says that he would do anything for Jesus. 'Lord, I am ready to go with you to prison and to death,' he declares. He means it too.

Jesus replies. 'I tell you, Peter, before the cock crows today, you will deny three times that you know me.'

Now we need to go to a garden. It's in the dark of the evening, Jesus asks Peter, James and John to go out with him. They find themselves in an olive grove called the Garden of Gethsemane.

'Pray that you will not fall into temptation,' Jesus says to his three friends before he goes a little ahead and kneels to pray. The disciples try to pray too but they're so tired, so very tired and stressed and confused. A voice wakens them.

'Why are you sleeping?' Jesus asks.

Peter, James and John feel upset. Peter had promised to do anything for Jesus, and here he is sound asleep just when Jesus is in need of him. Then things move fast!

Judas – one of the twelve disciples – arrives with a crowd of men. It takes Peter a minute to grasp what's happening. They are soldiers! They've come to arrest Jesus!

Judas leans forward to kiss Jesus. That's the sign that shows the soldiers which one to arrest. Peter reaches for his sword, swings it at one of the soldiers and cuts off his ear!

'No more of this,' Jesus says firmly, and then heals the man!

The disciples watch amazed, horrified, confused beyond words. Then Jesus is led away by the soldiers to the high priest's house. But Peter is not going to abandon Jesus. He would do anything for him.

Jesus is taken away for interrogation and Peter is determined to be near him in his time of trouble. It's late, it's dark and it's cold. A group of people gather around a fire in the courtyard of the high priest's house and Peter joins them in order to keep warm. His mind is racing. He's in shock.

Now imagine that you are an onlooker in the courtyard. There's a buzz about the place. You've heard that a new prisoner is arriving. You overhear some people gossiping in the firelight.

The one they call Jesus has been arrested. Have his followers been arrested too, someone wonders. You've heard of Peter, the fisherman who became a follower of Jesus. He has followed Jesus for three years, listening to his teaching and witnessing the healing miracles. You've heard that many who were sick and disabled have been healed by Jesus. You've heard the rumour that he has brought dead people back to life again. Someone has even told you that Jesus is the Son of God, the Saviour. Then you look around. A stranger has joined you and the others by the warmth of the fire.

Suddenly one of the servant girls is staring the stranger in the face.

'This man was with him,' she announces. You know she's talking about Jesus.

'Woman, I don't know him,' the stranger declares. You can see that he is afraid. Something makes you think that he is horrified at what he has just said. Who is this man you wonder? For a time the stranger tries to keep out of the glow of the fire so that his face isn't seen.

'You are one of them!' someone else says, a little while later.

'Man, I am not!' the stranger almost shouts.

Suddenly a voice rises above the others.

'Certainly this fellow was with him, for he is a Galilean.'

The stranger gets really angry. His eyes flash. 'Man! I don't know what you're talking about!'

Just then a cock crows. You hear it and so does the stranger. In the distance the one they call Jesus turns and looks straight at him. Their eyes meet and the man who was so angry now runs away.

You stop and think for a moment. Perhaps the others were right ... that stranger was one of Jesus' followers ... perhaps it was even Peter.

Outside the courtyard Peter is weeping, heartbroken. He has denied his Lord and he knows it. He is a miserable failure.

The days that follow are awful beyond words. Jesus is tried and sentenced to death. Peter had hoped that Jesus would be the great Saviour but his hopes are dashed to the ground. Then there's the crucifixion when Jesus, his friend, teacher, guide, his everything, is nailed to a cross and left there to die. For three long hours when Jesus is on the cross the sun fails and the world is dark. And that darkness mirrors the darkness in Peter's mind and heart. He had said that he would do anything for Jesus but then he denied him, and now Jesus is dead. Peter has a burden that he feels he will carry for the rest of his life.

But three days later Jesus' death is followed by his rising from the grave. Peter actually sees the empty grave with his very own eyes. Jesus is alive! Jesus IS alive! JESUS REALLY IS ALIVE! Then, wonder of wonders, Peter sees Jesus himself! He doesn't criticize Peter for denying him. He doesn't even mention it. Peter is overwhelmed with joy, excitement and wonder. But will Jesus ever really trust him again?

(This story is found in Matthew 26:47-75.)

BIBLE VERSE

While they were eating, Jesus took
bread, gave thanks and broke it,
and gave it to his disciples, saying,
'Take and eat; this is my body.'
Then he took the cup, gave thanks
and offered it to them, saying,
'Drink from it, all of you. This is
my blood of the covenant, which
is poured out for many for the
forgiveness of sins.'

Matthew 26:26-28

THE BREAKFAST BARBECUE

Take your imagination back in time to just after Jesus rose from the dead. It's a week or two later and Peter has seen him with his very own eyes. Peter's denial is bothering him. Having spent three years following Jesus, the disciples are not quite sure what to do now that he is not there all the time.

Now, because Peter is a fisherman and by the Sea of Tiberias, it seems natural to do some fishing. After all, he's a married man with a wife to keep. 'I'm going out to fish,' he calls to Thomas, Nathanael, James, John and two other friends.

'We'll go with you,' they say.

It's late in the evening and Peter and the others set out for a night's fishing. But there doesn't seem to be a fish in the sea and there are certainly none in their nets. All night long they throw the nets into the water, first on one side of the boat and then on the other.

The fishermen row in one direction and then sit for a while, letting the boat settle. Then they row in another direction but the fish must have seen them coming, for they've all swum away! They set out to try deeper water and then fish in the shallows near the shore. Nothing! If ever there was a wasted night, this is it.

Just as dawn breaks Peter sees a man on the shore. The man calls out to them. 'Friends, haven't you any fish?'

'No,' Peter shouts back, expecting that to be the end of the conversation.

'Throw your net on the right side of the boat and you'll find some,' replies the stranger.

Peter and the others look at each other, shrug, and then heave their nets over the right side of the boat.

All of a sudden there's a splashing and thrashing like they've never seen before. The sea to the right of the boat looks as if it's coming to the boil! Dorsal fins cut through the water, tails flip and fish jump and others come up, open-mouthed, for air. The disciples' mouths are open too, open in amazement!

There are seven strong men on the boat. They all haul at the net to land this extraordinary catch

... but they can't! Suddenly, it's as though Peter's eyes have been opened and he recognises the man on the shore.

'It's the Lord!' someone shouts.

Then, leaving the other six to land the fish, Peter grabs his clothes, jumps into the water and strides out for the shore! Thomas, Nathanael, James, John and the two others are left trying to prevent the weight of the fish in the nets from capsizing the boat. Eventually they give up the struggle and some of them row for the shore while the others hang on tightly to the net, dragging it to land behind the boat. They were less than 100 metres from shore when the shoal of fish swam into the net, but it must have seemed a very long way to drag that weight, especially after Peter left them to get on with it!

On shore there is no doubt at all that the man is Jesus. There he is, beside a bright little fire with some fish already cooking on it! Not only that, he has provided bread for breakfast too.

'Bring some of the fish you have just caught,' Jesus says.

Jesus is given the fish he asked for and then someone decides to count how many there are altogether. It's not easy counting fish for they are slithery creatures, but eventually everyone agrees that a grand total of 153 have been caught! Amazingly the nets, which are not made for huge catches like that, didn't break under the weight.

'Come and have breakfast,' Jesus tells them.

None of them dares ask who he is, for they all know that he's the Lord. Jesus takes the bread and gives it to them and does the same with the freshly cooked fish. After a whole night in the boat everyone is hungry and tired and breakfast is exactly what they need, especially one cooked for them by the Son of God.

On Fire

Peter's full name is Simon Peter so when Jesus speaks to him he says, 'Simon, do you truly love me more than these?'

Peter looks around him. Of course he loves Jesus more than the fish, more than the sea and more than his six friends.

'Yes, Lord,' he replies, 'You know that I love you.'

Jesus looks him in the eye. 'Feed my lambs,' he says.

Peter knows what Jesus means for he has heard him call himself the Good Shepherd. His lambs and his sheep are those who trust in him. Jesus is asking Peter to look after the new young Christian believers. He is so grateful that Jesus has a job for him to do. When he denied him three times Peter thought that he might never be trusted again, by anyone.

'Simon son of John, do you truly love me?' asks Jesus.

Peter is taken by surprise by the Lord asking the same question for a second time.

'Yes, Lord, you know that I love you.'

Jesus says, 'Take care of my sheep.'

Why did Jesus ask Peter a second time? Doesn't he believe him? Jesus speaks again.

'Simon son of John, do you love me?'

Peter feels hurt. How can Jesus possibly doubt that he loves him? He's spent three whole years with the Lord. But the memory of what happened in the firelight in the high priest's house comes back to trouble him. He remembers how the cock crowed after he had denied the Lord three times and how Jesus had looked over at him so sadly. But Peter *does* love him. Despite what he did, Peter really does love Jesus and he wants him to know it. 'Lord,' he says. 'You know all things; you know that I love you.'

Jesus said, 'Feed my sheep.'

Peter knows in his heart that Jesus has forgiven him and given him a job of work to do.

Jesus has something to say before Peter begins that job, and he says it there at the Sea of Tiberias as Peter sits by the dying embers of the campfire.

'I tell you the truth,' Jesus says, 'when you were younger you dressed yourself and went where you wanted; but when you are old you will stretch out your hands, and someone else will dress you and lead you where you do not want to go.'

Peter wonders what this means. It will be some time before he discovers that Jesus is telling him that he is going to be asked to keep that promise he made on the night on which Jesus was taken prisoner.

'Lord, I am ready to go with you to prison and to death.'

A day is coming when Peter will be led by others to prison and to death for his Christian faith.

Jesus says one more thing, 'Follow me!'

In the days and months that followed Peter's breakfast barbecue on the seashore I am sure that he would often think back to that early morning conversation. I wonder how long it was before he realised that he had denied Jesus three times, and three times Jesus asked if Peter loved him. Jesus, who knows everything, knew that Peter loved him, but it was Peter who needed to know it for sure.

(This story is found in John 21:15-25.)

TONGUES OF FIRE

The fire in this story marks a great historic event.

For forty days after Jesus rose from the dead he appeared on earth. During that time someone asks Jesus if the time has come for Israel to be restored. Israel has been under Roman rule and many Jews think that the Saviour, when he comes, will overthrow the Romans and make Israel an independent country once again. But Jesus has a much greater kingdom than one small country on earth.

'It is not for you to know the times or dates the Father has set by his own authority,' Jesus declares. And then he goes on to make a promise to his disciples. 'You will receive power when the Holy Spirit comes on you; and you will be my witnesses in Jerusalem, and in all Judea and Samaria, and to the ends of the earth.'

When Jesus finishes speaking an amazing thing happens. There, right before the eyes of the disciples, he is taken up to heaven and a cloud hides him from their sight! They watch as Jesus leaves them. Suddenly, two men dressed in white appear.

'Men of Galilee,' they say, 'why do you stand here looking into the sky? This same Jesus, who has been taken from you into heaven, will come back in the same way you have seen him go into heaven.' This is the last time the disciples see Jesus on earth, but they know they will see him again in heaven.

A short time later the disciples are in Jerusalem with many other friends of Jesus to celebrate the Jewish festival of Pentecost. This is one of the three feasts in the year that Jewish men are meant to celebrate together. The city is heaving with people. There are Jews from all around the Mediterranean Sea and beyond, as well as 'God-fearers,' men who were not born Jews but who believe in the one true God. It is amazing walking through Jerusalem listening to all the different languages that are being spoken.

When the day of Pentecost comes Jesus' friends all meet together. Suddenly they are aware of a sound, a most strange sound. It's like a wind blowing and it fills the whole house where the disciples are sitting! They have never known anything like it before. Then the strangest of all things happens. What looks like tongues of fire appear in the room, and the tongues of fire separate and rest on the heads of all who are there!

No one is burned but something happens, something that no words can describe. All of the disciples, even Peter who denied Jesus, are suddenly filled with God's Holy Spirit. The tongues of fire are a sign of his coming. Everyone is surprised and tries to talk about what is happening. Amazingly they find themselves all talking in different languages! God certainly is the God of surprises!

People passing by the house hear the commotion and before long a crowd gathers. It's most extraordinary. The friends of Jesus are all Hebrew-speaking. They are now in the middle of a great crowd of people who speak many different languages and they can all understand what the disciples are saying!

'Are these men not all from Galilee?' strangers ask each other. 'How can we all hear them in our own languages?'

Parthians, Medes and Elamites hear Jesus' friends speaking their languages. So do people from Mesopotamia, Judea and Cappadocia.

And that isn't all. The men who have come from Pontus and Asia also understand what is being said. So can those who have travelled from Phrygia and Pamphylia, Egypt and Libya. Even visitors all the way from Rome understand what Jesus' followers are saying! None of them have experienced anything like it.

'What does this mean?' the puzzled men ask.

Others are quick to be critical and say that the speakers are drunk. Have you ever heard of anyone who learned a new language just because he was drunk? He'd be more likely to forget words in his own language than do that!

But this is an opportunity not to be missed and Peter doesn't miss it. He stands up and speaks to the crowd. 'Fellow Jews and all of you who are in Jerusalem, let me explain this to you; listen carefully to what I say. These men are not drunk, as you suppose. It's only nine in the morning!'

Peter goes on to explain that God's Word says that his Holy Spirit will come to his servants, and that's what's happening. In fact, Peter, preaches a sermon about Jesus being the Son of God. 'God has made this Jesus, whom you crucified, both Lord and Christ.' When the people hear this, many ask what they should do.

Peter tells them, 'Repent, and be baptized, every one of you, in the name of Jesus Christ so that your sins may be forgiven. And you will receive the gift of the Holy Spirit. The promise is for you and your children and for all who are far off – for all whom the Lord our God will call.'

That day, when Peter finished speaking, about 3,000 people became Christians. The church was born. Peter had begun his special work for Jesus. He was feeding his lambs and his sheep.

(This story is found in Acts 2:1-41.)

UP IN FLAMES!

I hope you've never seen a riot close up; that would be scary. But you've probably seen riots on the television news. If you have, they will help you to picture our next destination. We are going a long way back in time, to a few years after the Lord Jesus died and went to heaven. Clear your mind and then try to picture the scene. Paul, who was a first-century missionary, spent over two years in Ephesus. To begin with he taught in the Jewish synagogue for about three months. After that, because those who attended the synagogue started saying bad things about Christianity, Paul moved to a lecture hall and held discussions there for two whole years.

Now, imagine you are in a large room and Paul is talking to a group of men about the Lord. Listen carefully and you hear many different accents and different languages too. You see, Ephesus is a seaport and travellers come and go all the time. No wonder God sends Paul to Ephesus for two years – travellers who hear the good news about the Lord Jesus will take it with them on their travels and tell others what they have heard!

Amazing things happen during this time. Picture yourself in the crowd in Ephesus as someone comes running with news. It's the most amazing news! A person who was ill was cured when he touched a handkerchief that Paul had touched! There are lots of stories about people being cured just like that. Maybe some superstitious men and women think that Paul is a magician. How wrong they are! People are only healed because God makes them better.

Where God is doing wonderful things, the devil is often at work too. That was true in Ephesus. Some Jews, who were not Christians, tried to do miracles.

When they met people who were possessed by evil spirits they said, 'In the name of Jesus whom Paul preaches, I command you to come out!' It wasn't just the occasional fraudster who tried that trick; one family of seven brothers were all at it! Believe it or not, they were the sons of the Jewish priest!

One day, when they commanded an evil spirit to come out of someone in the name of Jesus, they had a nasty surprise when the spirit spoke back to them!

'Jesus I know and Paul I know about, but who are you?' it demanded.

The demon-possessed man then jumped on the seven brothers and overpowered them all! The spirit had made the man very powerful indeed because he beat up all the brothers, ripped off their clothes and, when they escaped from the house, they were much the worse of the encounter.

Of course, when a dramatic event like that happens news travels very quickly indeed. Men and women began to realise that Jesus, who had died and risen again, was special, very, very special.

It was really difficult for young Christians in Ephesus at that time. It took a huge amount of courage to admit openly that you believed in

Jesus. But after the seven brothers were beaten up by the demon-possessed man, secret believers took courage and spoke openly about the bad things they'd done in the past. They told everyone that Jesus was their Saviour. That caused quite a stir!

There's more to come! Imagine the scene that follows. A number of people who have practised sorcery – that is witchcraft, and very evil in the eyes of God – bring together their spell books. These scrolls are very valuable because printing hadn't been invented and every one of them has been individually written by hand. It would have taken hours to write a book like that! Scribes charged for writing scrolls and only wealthy people ever owned any. So you can tell by the valuable scrolls that these men have made a very good living by witchcraft. They can afford to buy their own handwritten sorcery scrolls.

But these wealthy men are dumping their precious scrolls on the ground. They are no longer sorcerers but Christians! Now look what's happening. One of them is setting the pile alight! Before long the pile of wicked and evil scrolls is blazing. A crowd gathers round for the new Christians are courageous and want everyone to know what they are doing.

Someone did arithmetic after that famous fire. He calculated how much the scrolls were worth. The Bible tells us that they were worth 50,000 drachmas. A drachma was about what a man was paid for a day's work. So these sorcery scrolls were worth what a man would be paid for working six days a week for 159 years, 38 weeks and five days, which is the same as what 159 men would be paid for working six days a week for one year, one hour and twenty minutes. That was very serious money and everyone there knew it.

No doubt some people wanted to grab a scroll from the fire and sell it. Others, the Christians, would have thanked God that the former sorcerers were prepared to burn a fortune. They were so sure that Jesus was their Saviour. Others in the crowd would have been thinking that the people burning their scrolls were quite out of their minds.

Not long afterwards Paul, who had been preaching and teaching in Ephesus for over two years, decided that it was time to leave and go to Jerusalem. The church in Ephesus was young and the men and women, boys and girls were sad to hear that their minister was leaving. Remember, there were no phones in those days, or e-mails and letters took a very long time to arrive.

Just as the church in Ephesus was growing used to the idea of Paul going away, an extraordinary thing happened.

Imagine you are in the centre of Ephesus. You hear a man shouting. It's Demetrius the silversmith who makes idols. The idols are statues of the so-called goddess, Artemis, and are worth nothing more than the silver they are made from. Listen to what he's shouting. 'Men, you know that we receive a good income from this business. And you see and hear how this fellow Paul ... says that man-made gods are not gods at all. There is danger not only that our trade will lose its good name, but also that the temple of the great goddess, Artemis, will be discredited, and the goddess herself ... will be robbed of her divine majesty.'

All of a sudden, all around you, other silversmiths start shouting too.

'Great is Artemis of the Ephesians!' they roar, angry that they might lose their jobs.

It's becoming scary. There's shouting and screaming and stamping and raging! It goes on and on … and on … and on…. The noise all around you goes on for *two solid hours*! It only begins to calm down when the City Clerk demands that they be quiet and make any protest against Paul and his friends in a proper and legal way.

Eventually the riot is over and the crowd scatters to all the corners of the great city of Ephesus. Paul, some of whose friends have been dragged to the courthouse during the riot, gathers the Christians together. It's time for him to go. Sad

though the young church in Ephesus no doubt is, the Christians are so grateful that Paul is uninjured and free to tell others about the Lord Jesus Christ.

During the rest of Paul's life he must have had many hours on his own. Do you think his mind sometimes went back to Ephesus? When that happened, do you think he would remember the great riot there and the danger he was in? Or do you think he would remember the fire when keen young Christians, who used to be sorcerers, burned an absolute fortune in evil books?

(This story is found in Acts 18:8-22.)

BIBLE VERSE

One night the Lord spoke to Paul in a vision: 'Do not be afraid; keep on speaking, do not be silent. For I am with you, and no one is going to attack and harm you, because I have many people in this city.'

Acts 18:9-10

SIZZLING SNAKE!

The early Christians were in constant danger of their lives. Paul, one of the first missionaries, was often in serious trouble for teaching that Jesus is God and that he is the one and only way to heaven. More than once Paul was thrown in prison, eventually being tried in court in Jerusalem. But Paul was a Roman citizen and he demanded to be tried in Rome, the capital city of the Empire.

Imagine you set sail with him from Adramyttium on a ship large enough to carry 276 crew, along with passengers, prisoners and soldiers to guard the prisoners. Paul is guarded by an important soldier, a centurion. Centurions each command a hundred men. At first things go all right. You call at several Mediterranean ports and you can see the sailors are beginning to worry that it's getting past the time of year for crossing that great sea.

'We've lost so much time,' says one sailor to another.

'Yes,' his friend agrees. 'It's becoming dangerous.'

Paul hears the conversation.

'Men, I can see that our voyage is going to be disastrous and bring great loss to ship and cargo and to our lives also.'

The centurion is not impressed.

'The ship's pilot has agreed to continue the voyage,' he says. 'And the owner of the ship wants us to continue, so we will continue!'

The majority of those aboard go along with that opinion and they sail on, hoping to reach Phoenix and spend the winter there before continuing to Rome when the better weather comes again in springtime.

Soon the gentle south wind that has been blowing turns into a hurricane, a fierce north-easter. It catches the ship and drives it along at speed.

'Hoist the lifeboat aboard in case we lose it!' someone shouts.

The wind is so strong the men struggle to obey and only just manage to pull it on deck and tie it securely.

'Lower the sea anchor!' orders the captain, over the hurricane-force winds.

The sailors do as they're commanded, but the ship continues to be driven along.

'Throw the cargo overboard to lighten the ship!' the captain orders.

And still the storm blows.

Three days later, no doubt exhausted, there comes another ominous command.

'Throw the ship's tackle overboard!'

Things are getting desperate. For three days it's so dark that neither the sun nor the stars can be seen.

'Where are we?' sailors ask each other.

Nobody knows, for they sail by the stars and the stars are nowhere to be seen.

'Nothing can save us now,' someone wails.

Let's see what happened next.

Paul stands up, no doubt holding on tightly to keep himself from being blown overboard.

'Men, you should have taken my advice not to sail from Crete; then you would have spared yourselves this damage and loss. But now I urge you to keep up your courage, because not one of you will be lost; only the ship will be destroyed. Last night an angel of the God whose I am and whom I serve stood beside me and said, "Do not be afraid, Paul. You must stand trial before Caesar; and God has graciously given you the lives of all who sail with you." So keep up your courage, men, for I have faith in God that it will happen just as he told me. Nevertheless, we must run aground on some island.'

For the next fourteen days the ship battles against the storm. The crew are unable to steer and most of the time they have no idea what direction it's going in anyway.

On Fire

'I think we're getting near land,' a sailor shouts one day.

'Take a sounding!' the captain orders.

'We're at 37 metres,' the sailor who took the sounding yells over the storm.

'Its 27 metres now,' he shouts a little while later.

'We're going aground!' men scream from this direction and the other. 'The boat will smash to pieces.'

It's night time and dark as can be.

'Drop the anchors and pray for daylight,' the sailors are ordered.

Four anchors are dropped from the stern and then men pray for the morning to come.

In the dark one of the sailors nudges his friend. The noise of the wind is so loud no one hears what they are saying.

'Let's put the lifeboat down and get away from here before the sun rises. Nobody'll notice. They'll think we're putting down more anchors.'

But Paul notices.

'Unless these men stay with the ship,' he tells the centurion and the soldiers, 'you cannot be saved.'

The sailors watch, horrified, as the soldiers cut the ropes that hold the lifeboat and let it loose into the storm-tossed sea.

'For the last fourteen days,' Paul tells the crew, just before dawn breaks, 'you have been in constant suspense and have gone without food – you haven't eaten anything. Now I urge you to take some food. You will need it to survive. Not one of you will lose a single hair from his head.'

Having said that, Paul thanks God for his food in front of everyone on the boat, breaks the bread he's holding and has it for breakfast!

'Land ahoy!' sailor shouts to sailor as the sun rises.

They can see a bay with a sandy beach, but nobody knows where it is.

It's decision time and the captain makes it.

'Cut loose the anchors!'

The sailors cut the ropes that hold the anchors.

'Untie the rudders!'

Other sailors rush to obey, cutting the ropes that hold the rudders. They are now completely at the mercy of the storm.

'Hoist the foresail to the wind!'

Sailors heave the ropes that yank up the foresail and they are nearly torn from their hands as the wind catches the sail. What a struggle it is to secure it!

There's a sandbar between the ship and the beach and there's no way of avoiding it. Driven on by the force of the storm, the bow of the ship strikes the sandbar! The wooden ship heaves with the impact and sounds of cracking wood come from every direction. As the surf pounds its weary timbers the vessel begins to break up. The cracking and the crashing, the snapping and the smashing of the ship fills the air.

But then you see that the soldiers are unsheathing their weapons!

'What are you doing?' someone asks.

'We're going to kill the prisoners to stop them swimming to the island and escaping.'

'Stop it!' orders the centurion. He didn't want Paul killed.

The centurion took command. 'If you can swim, jump overboard and swim to the island. If you can't swim, grab a plank of wood and hold on to it for all you're worth. The surf will drive you ashore.'

And that's exactly what happens. Every sailor, every soldier and every single prisoner lands on the shore of the unknown island. They are all safe but utterly exhausted and very, very, wet!

The island is Malta. The locals are friendly and helpful and they rush to care for those who have suddenly landed on their beach.

'Build a fire!' someone shouts. 'These poor men are frozen as well as soaking.'

Paul, who is as tired as all the others, joins the search for wood. It isn't too long before the fire begins to burn and you are now standing in its warmth as it blazes brightly. Oh, the lovely warmth that's being given off now!

Paul arrives back with his arms full of wood and puts it right on to the fire. Suddenly everyone sees a viper wrapping itself round his arm! It was among the firewood and the flames drove it out. People scream in fear as they distance themselves from the poisonous snake.

'He must be a murderer!' one of the islanders says. 'Although he escaped from the sea, justice isn't going to let him live!'

But Paul shakes his wrist and the snake falls down into the flames!

'Watch!' you hear a voice say. 'His hand will swell up in a minute.'

'Either that or he'll drop down dead,' someone else announces.

All eyes are fixed on Paul. Only Paul's hand isn't swelling up. Paul isn't keeling over ... and he certainly isn't dead! The talk takes a different turn.

'Why didn't that man die from snake venom?' they ask each other.

'He must be a god!' someone suggests, and the others agree with that.

We can be absolutely sure that when Paul heard them say that, he made sure they understood that he was not a god. And he would certainly have told them about the one true and living God, the Father of our Lord Jesus Christ.

It was a further three months before Paul and the centurion left Malta and headed for Rome where he was to be put on trial once again.

No doubt the fire and the snake were still being talked about for a long time afterwards.

God is Sovereign and he reigns over all things. It was no mistake that Paul was involved in a shipwreck. It was no mistake that a snake attached itself to Paul's arm when he threw his wood on the fire. And it was no mistake that Paul was taken to Rome to be tried. We can't always see the reasons why things happen as they do, but we know God has his reasons. What we can see is that God used Paul's circumstances to help spread the good news about Jesus all around the Mediterranean area of the world.

(This story is found in Acts 27:1–28:10.)